VERMONT

a special world

Glover Porch, by Mack Derick

RALPH N. HILL/MURRAY HOYT/WALTER R. HARD, JR.

VERMONT

a special world

VERMONT LIFE MAGAZINE  MONTPELIER, VERMONT

Spring Run-off, by Hanson Carroll

Sugaring near Wilmington,
by John Harris

Sugaring, Jeffersonville, by Grant Heilman

White Tail at Bolton, by Bullaty-Lomeo

Mt. Mansfield from Jeffersonville, by Grant Heilman

Howe Bridge, Tunbridge, by John H. Vondell

Red Maple Buds, by Ernest Gay

West Windsor Hillside, by Robert Holland

All to the Borders

RALPH N. HILL

All the towns upon the lake Champlain and for three teer back the best sort of land. Not very heavy timbered, or stony or mountainous, well intersected with streams, and the streams full of small fish. Moose plenty on the mountains over against Jericho, Essex and Colchester. People hunt them in lieu of beef and get their tallow. Bears and wolves plenty. Beach, maple, pine, hemlock, cherry, birch and some oak and walnut. About 40 families in a town, about 40 towns totally unsettled. Land extraordinarily good from Rutland and Tinmouth clear to Canada line.

All sadly parsimonious, many profane, yet cheerful and much more contented than in Hartford [Connecticut], and the women more contented than the men, turned tawney by the smoke of the log-huts. Dress coarse and mean and nasty and ragged. Some very clever women and men, serious and sensible. Scarcely any sensible preaching. They were charmed with my sermons and my delivery and bestowed encomiums which it would be vain in me to repeat, such as the very first rate, philosophical, deep, penetrating, a great Scholar, angelic.

When I go from hut to hut, from town to town in the Wilderness, the people nothing to eat, to drink or wear, all work, and yet the women quiet, serene, peaceable, contented, loving their husbands, their home, wanting never to return, nor any dressy clothes; I think how strange! I ask myself are these women of the same species with our fine Ladies? Tough are they, brawney their limbs, their young girls unpolished and will bear work as well as mules. Woods make people love one another and kind and obliging and good natured. They set much more by one another than in the old settlements. Leave their doors unbarred. Sleep quietly amid flees, bedbugs, dirt and rags. O how vile, how guilty, how ungrateful to providence are our women! Tell lies about one another, envy one another, go abroad, dress and enjoy fine roads, carriages, husbands to wait on them, and are yet uneasy, unaffectionate!

I grieve to hear what thousands and thousands have endured in coming to this State of Vermont. One thing is now deeply affecting. The frowns of the Almighty are on this State for their sins. A famine is now felt in this land. Several women I saw had lived four or five days without any food, and had eight or ten Children starving around them, crying for bread and the poor women had wept till they looked like Ghosts.

I perform this day the office of physician and nurse to Mrs. Chittenden, who is very sick with a disorder called St. Anthony's fire. They seem to love me as a brother, and the Governor as a son. I struck them upon the right key. Queer is human nature and has a blind side. His Excellency picked me out to understand human nature at first sight.

About one quarter of the inhabitants and almost all the men of learning deists in the State. People pay little regard to the Sabbath, hunt and fish on that day. Not more than 1/6 part of the families attend family prayer in the whole State. About 1/2 would be glad to have the Gospel. The rest would chuse to have no Sabbath, no ministers, no religion, no heaven, no hell, no morality.

— *Nathan Perkins, 1789*

black bear or perhaps a full grown bruin. In another a fiddler draws his bow vehemently, throwing out sounds rasping and loud which are nearly drowned in the din and hurly-burly without. At another the proprietor stands vociferating to the passing throng: "walk up, call up, roll up, tumble up, any way to get up." The refreshments having been disposed of, the green is covered with straggling masses where there is wrestling, jumping and other trials of strength. Peddlers mount their carts, and by loud shouting and wild gesticulation attract an eager throng to whom they vend cheap wares at auction. The inevitable soapman is here too with his jokes and songs. The liberated soldiers are gay and frolicsome.

The recess ends, and the drum-major in scarlet coat and with official baton, draws up his corps of fifes and drums, and the long roll sounds. Officers and men hurry back to their places and the afternoon exercises commence. The troops march through the streets and the town is enlivened with the shrill notes of the fifes and the rub-a-dub of the drums. After this comes inspection, when the arms and equipment of each individual soldier are carefully examined and noted upon the orderly book.

— *L. L. Dutcher, 1871*

Ho! all to the borders, Vermonters come down.
With your breeches of deer-skin and jackets of brown,
With your red woolen caps and your moccasins, come
To the gathering summons of trumpet and drum.
Come down with your rifles, let gray wolf and fox
Howl on in the shade of their primitive rocks,
Let the bear feed securely from pig-pen and stall,
Here's a two-legged game for your powder and ball.
Leave the harvest to rot on the field where it grows,
And the reaping of wheat to the reaping of foes,
Our vow is recorded, our banner unfurled,
In the name of Vermont, we defy all the world.

— *John G. Saxe, 1864*

South Londonderry, by John Harris

Dawn on the Ottauquechee and
Mt. Ascutney in Spring, by Robert Holland

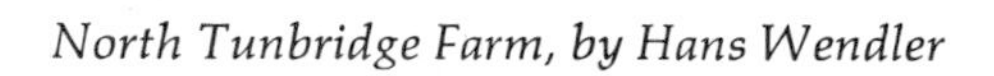

North Tunbridge Farm, by Hans Wendler

Marlboro Birches,
by John H. Vondell

Pomfret Apple Blossoms,
by Winston Pote

Country Home, Williamsville, by John H. Vondell

Fishing the Battenkill, by Hanson Carroll

East Corinth, by Hans Wendler

Opening Day Ritual

MURRAY HOYT

There are Vermonters to whom, quite simply, Springs means trout fishing. To these fine, dedicated individuals Opening Day is sacrosanct. They train their wives early that unimportant matters like jobs, responsibilities, relatives, anniversaries and the like must never be allowed to interfere with the reverent solemnization of this annual event.

The spring after my marriage in the early nineteen-thirties I inaugurated such a wife-training program. For the site of my Opening Day operations I chose the East Middlebury River, at the foot of the Green Mountains.

The only drawback was that Marg, my wife, needed the car. However, a good resourceful trout fisherman who has made up his mind to go fishing is seldom stymied by so trivial a matter as this. We decided that Marg would drive me over to the stream and then go about her business. Late in the day she would return and pick me up.

We rose while it was still dark and unbelievably cold. We ate breakfast, made me a couple of sandwiches, and started out. I wanted to be on the stream with the first streaks of dawn.

I fished for a while and got nothing. It was way too cold for trout fishing (or anything else), but as I've said, Opening Day is a ritual.

It was so cold that there was a skimming of ice on the stagnant water at the bottom of the big pools. It was so cold that ice built up on the line, and inside the guides. of the rod. You couldn't fish decently with gloves on, and your fingers got numb if you fished without gloves. You got to shaking because you needed at least two more sweaters than you already had on.

But I had the day to spend, and it was Opening Day, and I tried. I knocked the ice off the guides, and stripped it off the line. I fished grimly.

I came to a deep pool where I had always had good luck. It eddied against a sloping rock. I dropped the worm into the eddy — I was using worms since no fly in his right mind would hatch out under such conditions, and no fish in his right mind would venture up after him if he did — and steered it through the eddy carefully.

I reached out to bring it around just right, and suddenly I felt my feet going out from under me. The moss and the rock had been wet, and the wet had frozen into some of the slipperiest ice it has ever been my bad fortune to encounter.

I sat down hastily and grabbed at everything in the neighborhood. Nothing I could get my hands on had any permanency. I began to slide, slowly at first, the way a giant tree starts its fall under the woodman's ax. Then faster and faster.

Clawing and breaking fingernails on everything near me, I slid majestically into the pool.

I have heard it said that under these conditions your boots, full of water, will weight you down and pull you under and drown you. That drowning bit didn't appeal to me at all. I set myself for the shock of going under and to the bottom. I prepared myself to walk on the bottom if it was necessary, until I could get the short distance to where my head would poke out.

The shock never came. I never got really under. The straps on my boots were pulled tight around my legs, and a lot of air was trapped inside my heavy pants and my jacket and all the clothes I had on.

I went under only about halfway between my waist and my armpits. For one split second I didn't even feel the water until it got through all that clothing. When it did, *that* was a shock, believe me.

I was buoyed up there by all that air like a fat old lady with an innertube around her. I couldn't even start swimming the way you normally would. I had to reach down to paddle. As more and more water got inside and dispelled the air, I sank lower and lower. But the shore was only a few yards distant. Majestically, sticking up there like a cork, I floated myself over to it and waded out.

Obviously this was a sticky situation. I had no car, it was miles to a telephone. Besides, I wanted to fish.

I repaired to the most sheltered place I could find. I took off my boots first and that wasn't easy. Did you ever try to take off a pair of boots half-full of water? The water forms some sort of vacuum and the resulting suction makes the task fit right along with getting your leg out of a quicksand.

I then took off the socks, the jackets, the sweaters, and the longhandled underwear. After that I stood there in that icy morning air, just as I had been when the doctor held me upside down and slapped my bottom, only larger and right side up.

I emptied out the boots. Then I started wringing everything else out. I wrung every last drop out that I could for two reasons; I wanted it out of there, and wringing it hard kept my blood circulating.

I got myself as dry as I could, and I put everything back on. It was unbelievably cold and clammy at first, but my body warmed things up shortly. And at least the clothes acted as wet insulation.

I went back to fishing, testing all rocks for ice before I trusted myself to them. I still had miserable luck. I might very well be catching cold, but it was a cinch I wasn't catching anything else.

Then I met a friend of mine named Ed. He had had the same luck I had had, but he was dry.

"What we need to do is fish a lake," he told me. "In a lake the water temperature wouldn't have dropped as low with this sudden freeze, after the good weather we've been having. What do you say we try Lake Pleiad?"

I didn't mention that I felt I was an authority on the water temperature of that particular brook. I said, "I got no car."

"Come with me."

We drove up the mountain on Route 125. As we neared the top there began to be snow beside the road. Right below Lake Pleiad is nowadays the Middlebury Snow Bowl ski area, and it will have maybe fifty inches of snow up there when there won't be any down in Middlebury.

We had taken for granted that with the warm spring we'd had, all snow up there would be gone. We'd been pretty naïve.

"Anyhow, we can hike through the snow for the half a mile in there. It will be worth the hike to get some fish."

We found that the cold of the night before had made a crust atop some four feet of snow on the Trail. You'd take three steps on the crust, and when you took the fourth step your leg would go through and drop practically the length of it. If you weren't on the alert, this would snap your head forward like the knot on the end of a whip.

You'd retrieve your leg, go a couple more steps. And just when you were lulled into a false sense of security, the other leg would drop in and your head would snap again, jarring your teeth and maybe making you bite your tongue.

We traveled a long, long half-mile in this manner, buoyed up only by the thought of the fine fishing that awaited us.

As we traveled we developed a cunning in that matter of neck-snapping. If you held your neck constantly rigid enough, it lessened the snap. But it gave you a headache right then. And we later found that it made your neck sore for about four days afterward.

There was, too, one other little matter I had to contend with but that Ed didn't. When you have wrung out your clothing and put it back on, you can never get all the water out. It's impossible. So a drop here and a drop there, from your socks, your pants, your shirts and sweaters, and that heavy underwear, finds its way down into the bottom of your boots by force of gravity.

Ordinarily this isn't bad. Your body heat warms it up, and it isn't too uncomfortable. But when, every few steps, your boot goes into snow all over, snow packs around it, immediately the water inside starts to cool down like champagne in an ice bucket. When your legs aren't deep in snow, snow is clinging to the outside of your boot, and the sole of the boot is on crust.

By the time we were halfway in there, I was walking in a quart or more of ice water. To a person reading in a nice warm room with his feet dry, this may not seem like much of a disaster. Let me assure you there is nothing quite like it in the world for exquisite torture. The Inquisition would most certainly have used it if they'd thought of it or if they'd been able to pick up a pair of hip boots and four feet of snow.

But I buoyed myself, as I say, with anticipation.

And then we made the last turn in the trail, and Lake Pleiad lay there before us — a solid sheet of ice. Not just anchor ice. This was the winter's solid stuff. It never had melted up high that way, as we had assumed it had; the way all the lakes down in the valley had melted long since.

We never wet a line. You couldn't have, short of owning an ice chisel. And then there was the trek out with the boot water getting nearer and nearer thirty-two degrees. I felt like yelling out loud under the torture.

I sat on the car seat with my legs stuck out while Ed worried my boots off for me. I wrung out the socks again and the bottoms of my trousers, and put everything back. I felt better after that. We drove back down into the valley.

It was still only about nine-thirty in spite of all that had happened. We began to fish the huge pool at Big Bend.

No luck. The long rock at the head of the pool was comfortable though, and we were loath to leave the place. Our stomachs had for some time back been assuring us with more and more authority that our watches were wrong and that noon had come, so we broke out a sandwich apiece. While I was wringing some of the water out of my sandwiches and the rest of my lunch, Ed let the current carry his worm deep into the pool. And when it stopped and would go no further, he laid the rod down beside him on the rock and we attacked the sandwiches. Ed ate his and I drank mine.

When we were ready to start on, Ed began to reel in. There was a pleasant tugging at the end of his line, and he landed an eleven-inch brookie.

He threw back, and I threw in my line. Nothing happened. We just sat there. After a long time I felt a tug, and I landed a nice brookie. Ed landed one shortly thereafter.

So we settled ourselves on the rock and just allowed our baits to lie on the bottom where the current deposited them. They'd stay there quite a few minutes, then there'd be a bite.

Ed said, "Looks like all the fish in this pool are in one bunch, and we're letting our bait lie there among 'em until looking at it makes even a half-frozen trout hungry."

I'd never fished brookies that way before. But we hadn't found any fish biting anywhere else, so we just sat there. And the fish kept on coming in — not fast, but steadily. The black clouds in the sky increased; we fished on.

You'd be surprised how rapidly fish mount in your creel under such circumstances. The limit at that time was twenty. We passed ten each and it began to snow. Still we sat there.

When we reached twenty apiece it was snowing hard.

I now had my limit, and it was still morning. Marg wasn't due till after five o'clock that afternoon. Somehow I couldn't cozy up to the idea of sitting around there nearly six hours in a blinding snowstorm, my clothes wet below the armpits.

So I cadged a ride into Middlebury with Ed. And from Middlebury I started to walk toward Addison, where the car would be. It's nine miles from Middlebury to Addison.

I walked. I walked and walked. The boots, and some more seeped-down water in them, got heavier and heavier. Both heels began to chafe in the wet socks and the spots got to feeling as if somebody were holding a match against them. When you're walking a brook to fish, you don't even think about it. When you're walking just to get somewhere, you think about nothing else.

The twenty brook trout in the creel, which had at first seemed only pleasantly heavy, went rapidly through various stages until I'd have sworn each fish was eight times its size and made of lead.

I walked six miserable miles, and only the first one held itself down to a mere 5,280 feet. I got a ride the last three miles, and only the fact that the driver who stopped and picked me up was sitting in his car kept me from dropping to my knees and kissing his feet.

But the strange part is that after I got dry, and the blisters healed, I found that I'd had a wonderful time. I wouldn't have missed it for the world. In the years to come it took its place as one of the nicest days I ever spent. This doesn't seem either reasonable or sensible. But that's how it was.

Dorset Mt.,
by Arthur Griffin

A Manchester Brook, by John Harris

A Yellow Towhee Sings in a Budded Tree and a Grosbeak and a Scarlet Tanager perch in new Leaves, by Ernest Gay

Moss Glen Falls, Granville Gulf, by Dick Smith

Cilley Bridge, Tunbridge, by Lud Munchmeyer

A Field of Golden Dandelions in Wilmington and a Country Road South of Arlington, by H. Stanley Johnson

Fishing in Marshfield, by Bruce O. Nett

Pownal View, by Carsten W. Johnson

Bee and Apple Blossoms, by Ernest Gay

Warren,
by David Witham

You are the Guardians

WALTER R. HARD, JR.

The peculiar beauty of Vermont's countryside, first described in 1609 by Samuel Champlain, has occupied writers for a full quarter-millennium since. And for the past two centuries others have been trying to explain the enigma of the people who lived here. Vermont has been recognized nationally for its singular and hypnotic charm, so it is natural, perhaps, that its outward look in very recent years has become the growing concern of many who want to keep it from submersion by megalopolis and from being modernized to the point of ruin.

The nature of the Vermonters themselves, their recognizable characteristics, appear to have undergone even greater, perhaps irrevocable, changes than their surroundings. Beginning in the Great Depression period, these observers, many of them speaking from a distaste for the other America, expressed their concern that the old Vermont way of life was largely changing or dying out.

Sinclair Lewis in 1929 was perhaps the first to say it, and oddly enough the author of *Babbitt* chose the Rotary Club at Rutland as his sounding board:

". . . I have found in Vermont precisely the opposite of the peculiar thing, pointed out and boasted of as 'very American'; the desire for terrific speed and the desire to make things grow.

"I like Vermont because it is quiet, because you have a population that is solid and not driven mad by the American mania — that mania which considers a town of 4,000 twice as good as a town of 2,000, or a city of 100,000, fifty times as good as a town of 2,000. Following that reasoning, one would get the charming paradox that Chicago would be ten times better than the entire state of Vermont, but I have been in Chicago, and have not found it so.

"I like your valleys and quiet towns — and Vermont is not yet bisected by cement roads 100 feet wide, lined by hot dog stands.

"Right now I can visualize a great New York syndicate holding a meeting. Somebody will mention Vermont. Probably members of the syndicate will say, 'yes, Vermont, *let's* go up there and be benefactors — build a 3000-room hotel on Mt. Ascutney . . .'

"It is hard in this day, in which the American tempo is so speeded up, to sit back and be satisfied with what you have. It requires education and culture to appreciate a quiet place, but any fool can appreciate noise. Florida was ruined by that mania. It must not happen in Vermont.

"You have priceless heritages — old houses that must not be torn down, beauty that must not be defiled, roads that must not be cluttered with billboards and hot dog stands. You are the guardians — and you are fortunate to have the honor of that task instead of being hornblowers."

This Rutland trailblazer apparently provoked little discussion at the time of its delivery. But Lewis's wife, the celebrated journalist Dorothy Thompson, had her assertion, that the Vermont hill farm life was "statistically bankrupt", picked up by Senator George D. Aiken, then Vermont's governor, in a spirited defense of rural living. Fiscally sound or not, Aiken wrote, "I hope the time will never come when the hills, submarginal land or otherwise, will be closed to occupancy as homes."

"Why do folks live in the hills?" [when the

It just happened that Mr. Lake had some pure-bred Jerseys that he'd let him have.

For a while Mr. Matthews spent his evenings in the barn making repairs so the cattle could be taken care of. This was on top of the mail deliveries. After the cattle arrived Mr. Matthews spent considerable time getting the hang of the milking machine. He had to get up by six in the morning to get the morning milking done ahead of going to the Post Office.

After he'd been carrying the mail about ten days one of the Post Office workers said, "How's the mud?"

Mr. Matthews said, "It's drying up. I got through fairly early today."

The man nodded. "Then Mr. Stebbins will be getting well any day now."

"You mean . . . . ?"

Mr. Stebbins returned two days later. He said he was on the road to recovery. "But I've had a bad siege. A bad one." He shook his head lugubriously.

Unfortunately the end of Mr. Matthews' postal duties did not spell rest for him. He attacked the garden. There was a lot more work with cows than he'd dreamed there could be. The lawn began to grow green and long.

In June haying started — he had to have hay for the winter needs of his cows — and the weeds in both his flower and his vegetable garden grew much faster than the items he had planted. By that time he had a considerable amount tied up in a tractor and haymaking equipment.

In July the garden began to bear copiously. And Mrs. Matthews, assisted by Mr. Matthews, was forced into canning and freezing the product of Mr. Matthew's labors. The church suddenly became more demanding. The Chamber of Commerce work doubled.

Also the Matthews started having company. Their friends from New York, some of whom they hadn't really known very well, became very interested in them and arrived. Mrs. Matthews found it very difficult to get away from the kitchen at all.

One night Mr. Matthews found that one of the cows had cut herself rather badly. And so Mr. Matthews got Mrs. Matthews to come out to the barn to hold the cow's head.

The job was somewhat gory, so that after some time Mrs. Matthews said suddenly, "Oscar, I'm going to faint."

Mr. Matthews said, "Please, Grace, we're almost through. Just hold Nellie's head a little longer. When we're through you can faint all you want to."

There were some moments of silence, and then a heavy Whock! Mrs. Matthews, in the face of Mr. Matthews' express orders, had fainted right then.

It was found her left ankle was broken, and she was taken to the hospital. Mr. Matthews now had her work added to his own. About the middle of the third day he keeled over and they took him to the same hospital Mrs. Matthews was patronizing. The doctor said he was suffering from extreme exhaustion.

"You'll have to be very quiet. No work at all. It would be best if you could retire and live in some quiet place in the country where you could get a complete rest."

"But I *am* retired," Mr. Matthews told him. "That's what started all the trouble."

"Then you'd better go back to work. Anything so that you'll take it easier."

After they sold the cows and turned the garden over to a neighbor, and hired a man, and resigned from everything but the church, Mrs. Matthews forgave Mr. Matthews and now they are back at home.

— *Murray Hoyt*

summer

Atop Mt. Mansfield, by Clyde Smith

Peacham Village, by Winston Pote

Floating Bridge, Brookfield, by Arthur Griffin

Gulls in Flight, Lake Champlain, by Bullaty-Lomeo

Morning Mist, Waterbury, by John H. Vondell

Heron in a Bog near Bradford, by Charles C. Johnson

Otter Creek Valley from the Landgrove to Mt. Tabor Road and a view from the top of Bromley to Stratton Mt., by Ernest Gay

Camel's Hump from the Molly Stark Balcony, Long Trail, by John H. Vondell

Tree Swallow, by Ernest Gay

Long Shadows on Hazen's Notch near Lowell, and Dusk at Joe's Pond, West Danville, by Bullaty-Lomeo

Buswell's Pond, Plymouth, by Richard Frutchey

They Settled the Hills

RALPH N. HILL

About eleven o'clock in the morning we set out [from Crown Point] with a fair wind. On both sides of the lake are high chains of mountains. On the eastern shore is a low piece of ground covered with a forest, extending between nine to twelve English miles, after which the mountains begin, and the country beyond them belongs to New England. This chain consists of high mountains, which are to be considered as the boundaries between the French and English possessions in these parts of North America.

The lake at first is but a French mile broad but keeps increasing in size afterwards. The country is inhabited within a French mile of the fort, but after that it is covered with a thick forest. At a distance of about ten French miles from Fort St. Frédéric, the lake is four such miles broad and we perceived some islands in it. This day the sky was cloudy and the clouds, which were very low, seemed to surround several high mountains near the lake with a fog. From many mountains the fog rose, as the smoke of a charcoal kiln. Now and then we saw a little river which emptied into the lake.

We often saw Indians in bark boats close to the shore, which was, however, not inhabited, for the Indians came here only to catch sturgeons wherewith this lake abounds and which we often saw leaping up into the air. These Indians lead a very singular life. At one time of the year they live on the small store of corn, beans, and melons which they have planted; during another period, or about this time, their food is fish, without bread or any other meat; and another season they eat nothing but game such as stags, roes, beavers, etc., which they shoot in the woods and rivers. They, however, enjoy long life, perfect health, and are more able to undergo hardships than other people. They sing and dance, are joyful and always content, and would not for a great deal exchange their manner of life for that which is preferred in Europe.

— *Peter Kalm, 1749*

In the course of this summer I took a singular stroll. I took six days of provisions in my pack, a small pocket pistol, little horn of powder, and a hatchet of a small size for the benefit of making fire, and set out to view the country a little to the North of Hubbardton. One evening I had made a fire and as there appeared a prospect of rain I had cut some crotches and stretched my blanket to keep off the rain, and cut some hemlock boughs for a bed, and laid down for repose, when I was soon disturbed by hearing thunder at a distance, preceded by the roaring of a tremendous wind. The falling of trees was incessant and I found the hurricane was coming directly to me. I had little time for consideration. I recollected seeing a large pine that was turned up by the roots, and at about eight feet lay firm on the ground, a safe retreat if all the trees in the woods were turned up by the roots. I had possession of my new habitation when the wind, rain, thunder and lightning reached the place. A great many trees and branches of trees were brought to the ground and some fell on every side of my fire. One tree fell across the log under which I lay a little distance from me. The storm was soon over. I repaired my fire and slept very comfortably the remainder of the night.

Two days after the hurricane I ascended a high

precipice or top of a mountain east of a long pond, the source of Hubbardton River in said town, where I found a great prospect to view the adjoining country. The day being clear and air pure contributed much to my prospect of learning from the top of a tall spruce tree, which stood within thirty feet of a ledge I judged to be at least 300 feet perpendicular. I had a small compass in my pocket and hatchet in my hand and climbed to the top of the tree. With the hatchet I cut off the top and trimmed it to answer as a compass staff, and placed my compass on it, turning and viewing lands at a great distance. While thus amusing myself, the day being some windy, a sudden gust of wind caused the top of the tree to wave over the ledge. At this unlucky moment I chanced to cast my eyes down the tree, waved by the wind over. It had the appearance that I was going to the bottom. This gave me sensations not easily expressed. Let it suffice to say it caused a general chill to the motion of the blood — a strong feeling in my head and heart, with weakness in my limbs, at which prudence dictated to me to put the compass instantly into my pocket, and go down the tree. I went about two thirds down, stopped, and, on a few minutes reflection, came to my usual feelings. I then considered that the wind was not so high as at many other times, that I must be unlucky indeed if the tree fell in the time necessary for me to take minutes of the lands in the adjacent country. I resumed my courage and went and set my compass on the top of said tree, and with my pen made regular minutes of my discoveries without looking down till my business was finished. From such a view I could gain as much general knowledge of the country as by a week's traveling through the low lands.

The fifth day of my stroll I was on the top of another high ledge. After climbing a tree and viewing the country I came down and discovered a large stone I could easily roll off, which for amusement I did, and several others. A little down the side of the first mentioned steep part of the rock lay a rock twice as big as a hogshead, and apparently easily turned off. I viewed it for some time and then ventured down, taking off my shoes. I was very cautious observing small bushes that grew out of the cracks of the rocks, and one just by the stone I wished to roll. I went back and cut two pries, there being a place I could put them under, and put my feet on the ends, so that I made use of both strength and heft to turn the rock off. By this means I turned it. A craggy piece of the rock that projected towards me, and which I took hold of when the rock moved, came against me as I was stooping over it lifting, and came near throwing me over the rock. I, by exertion, extracted myself, caught by the large bush aforesaid, and staid quiet where I was. But the danger I had escaped greatly eclipsed my pleasure in seeing the rock roll. But it went with tremendous force; and striking other rocks in its descent, raised a strong sulphurous smell, and when it came to the standing timber it cut its way like a bush scythe, carrying with it the butts of trees, their tops falling up the hill. This would have been a pleasant sight to me on a safe ground. I moved carefully to the top of the hill, and have been extremely careful in rolling rocks from such heights ever since.

— *Ira Allen, 1772*

Vermont has been settled entirely from the other States of New-England. In the formation of Colonies those who are first inclined to emigrate are usually such as have met with difficulties at home. These are commonly joined by persons who, having large families and small farms, are induced for the sake of settling their children comfortably to seek for new and cheaper lands. To both are always added the discontented, the enterprizing, the ambitious, and the covetous.

A considerable part of all who begin the cultivation of the wilderness may be denominated foresters or Pioneers. The business of these persons is no other than to cut down trees, build log-houses, lay open forested grounds to cultivation, and prepare the way for those who come after them. These men cannot live in regular society. They are too idle, too talkative, too passionate, too prodigal, and too shiftless to acquire property or character. They are impatient of the restraints of law, religion, and morality; grumble about the taxes by which Rulers, Ministers, and Schoolmasters are supported; and complain incessantly, as well as bitterly, of the extortions of mechanics, farmers, merchants, and physicians; to whom they are always indebted. After displaying their own talents and worth, after censuring the weakness and wickedness of their superiours, they become at length discouraged, and under the pressure of poverty, the fear of a gaol, and the consciousness of public contempt, leave their native places and betake themselves to the wilderness.

— *Timothy Dwight, 1810*

In great contrast to this extensive open forest land [of the hills] was the tangled wilds that overspread the valleys of the streams. There everything looked dark and peculiarly forbidding. There the evergreens of black timber such as hemlock, spruce and fir prevailed, and were thickly intermingled with birch, ash and elm; while a heavy and almost impervious growth of all sorts of underbrush gave the whole the appearance of a black, gloomy and impassable mass of woods. And besides this these tangled forests were found, when land-lookers or others succeeded in penetrating them, to be often so wet and swampy as to deter most emigrants from any attempt to clear them up for settlement. What wonder then that they so generally preferred to make drier pitches on the higher grounds. As the event proved, however, in clearing up the whole country, the settlers greatly underrated the value and feasibility of the low lands. For when the sun was once let in, and these dark masses of forest and the roots and stumps were rotted, the lowlands made beautiful, easy-wrought and productive meadows.

It now seems a singular fact that the first settlers of this State should have so generally pitched on the highest plains and plateaus, miles from any water power, for villages which they evidently supposed must become centres of population and seats of public business. A few of these upland villages, like Randolph Centre, Peacham and Danville, have made shift to retain there the locations of meeting-houses and academies, but that seems to have been about all. Their populations have been stationary or decreasing, while their business has nearly all gone down to the banks of the nearest rivers where thriving villages have sprung up, all seeming to begin alike and grow by the same natural process. In the first place a grist-mill and saw-mill were found to be matters of indispensable necessity. These of themselves became unavoidably places of resort and most favorable for seeing people from all other parts of the town. Hence soon followed the shoemaker, blacksmith, and soon the tavern-keeper and the merchant. And the nucleus of a village being thus formed, the place at once began to draw away the population of the hill village and grow to an important place of business. Such has proved so often the case that it may now be considered a settled matter that no village can long sustain itself or become a place of much importance located far aloof from good water-power.

— Daniel P. Thompson, circa 1870

Upper Hollow, Strafford, by Hanson Carroll

Early Morning near North Troy, by Grant Heilman

The McLam Farm, East Topsham, by Hanson Carroll

Round Barn, East of Lowell,
by Grant Heilman

Mt. Abraham from Lincoln,
by John F. Smith

Pownal Valley, by Carsten W. Johnson

Rolling Farm Lands North of Randolph and, left, near Stowe, by Carlos Elmer

Barn Painting in Wilmington, by John Harris

That's How It Was

MURRAY HOYT

A sweet young thing in her early teens said to me this summer, "Mr. Hoyt, *you* must remember way, *way* back when there was just nothing interesting going on in the world; no outer space program, no television, no radio even, no cars, no fast boats or water skiing, no tractors, no movies, no running-water, no plumbing, just *nothing*."

"Would you believe," I asked her, "that George Washington and I used to commiserate with each other about that very situation?"

And she said, "Oh, *you*! But seriously, whatever did people *do*? How did they get around? Especially way up here in Vermont away from everywhere? And with nobody earning much money?"

I went home and thought about this a lot. Several generations have come along whose members have no first-hand knowledge of what life with low earnings and without modern inventions was like. They feel sorry for us, probably rightly, for having been born too soon.

So this, Virginia, is my attempt to show you how awful it really was.

Beginning when I was two years old, I spent my summers with my family on Lake Champlain in our cottage at Potash Bay. Today there are two dozen or more cottages along the shores of Potash Bay, but at that time ours was the only one. It was set on corner rocks and was made of novelty siding on studding. There was no road to it; we had to reach it through a gate and along the edge of a hayfield. The gate had to be kept closed for fear cows might get into the meadow and trample the hay. The trip through the hayfield was about a quarter of a mile.

Barnet, by Winston Pote

The cottage had a huge screened porch on which my parents and I did most of our living and where we slept at night. There was a large living room with fireplace, a tiny kitchen, and four bedrooms upstairs. The plumbing wasn't. Its place was taken by a small building known by the somewhat less-than-frank title of "woodshed". Lake water was forced up into a storage tank on the second floor by a one-manpower pump, and from there reached a single faucet in the kitchen below by gravity. Any hot water was heated on the kitchen oil stove in a teakettle.

Similar cottages along Potash Bay today are sold at a figure between five thousand and ten thousand dollars. In 1907 my parents had spent the then magnificient sum of $100 to build these buildings.

I thought, very simply, that it was paradise. My father had been born and spent his boyhood near that cottage, but by that time he was the head of the English Department at Clark University. Therefore we lived in Worcester, Massachusetts during the school year.

For weeks before our leaving Worcester for the summer I planned and dreamed of the camp and the lake, and I'd pack fishing tackle and other things that mattered, days in advance of our scheduled departure.

We got up very early on the chosen morning, and rode on a trolley to Union Depot where we boarded the train for Winchendon. At Winchendon we changed to the Boston section of the rather optimistically titled "Green Mountain Flyer"

My father always found two green plush-cushioned seats together and turned over the

Hiking Atop Mt. Mansfield, by John H. Vondell

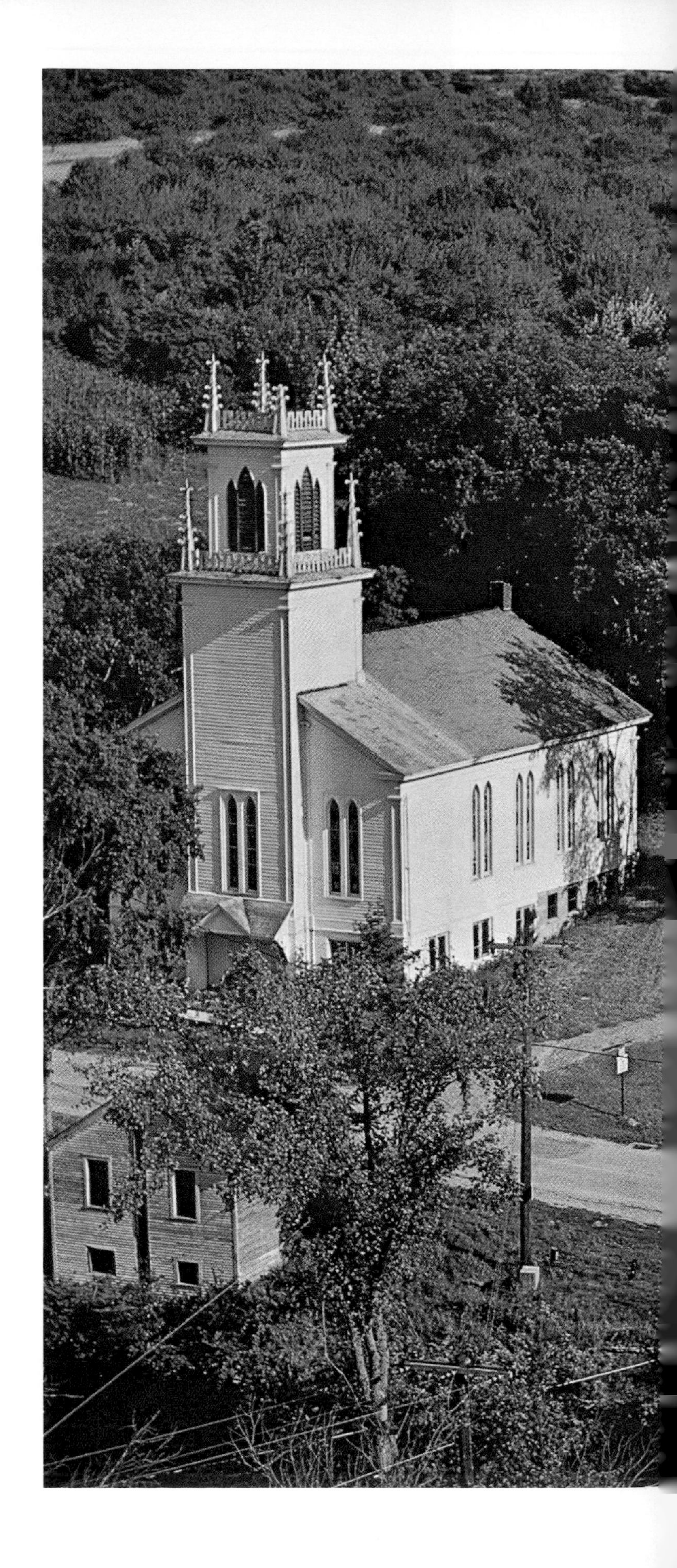

Lazy Summer Day in Pawlet, by Clyde Smith

ANDRUS

South Wardsboro Reflections,
by John Harris

Indian Paint Brush, West Dover,
by Lawrence McDonald

Middlebury Congregational Church,
by John F. Smith

Cycling through Lower Waterford and a
Sailing Race on Lake Champlain, near Shelburne, by Hanson Carroll

Connecticut River at Fairlee, by Ruth Archer

A Farm near Passumpsic, by Jack Breed

Tree Farm, West Woodstock, by David Witham

Sugarhouse in Cambridge, by Robert Hagerman

Factory Brook, Barnet,
by David Witham

Autumn's Bright Harvest

RALPH N. HILL

After dinner we set out for Manchester and, having rode two miles, were obliged to shelter ourselves from a violent rain in a saddler's shop. Here we continued till sun set and then returned to the inn at which we had dined. The building stood on a handsome elevation overlooking an extensive valley toward the East, and gave us a full prospect of the Green Mountain range for a great distance.

The wind blew violently from the North West. The heavens were dark; the clouds were wild, tossed in fantastical forms. Many of them struck the mountains at their middle height and thence sailed up their bosom with a motion which, notwithstanding their rapid progress over our heads, was to our eyes, slow, majestic, and awful. The world was universally wrapt in gloom and the bosom of the mountain was covered with a deep brown, approaching to black. After this melancholy and cavern-like darkness had continued about one hour; and tempest and tumult appeared to reign universally, suddenly most beautiful and brilliant spots of gold of various figures and sizes formed by the light of the sun piercing through the interstices of the clouds, were seen wandering over the surface of the valley beneath; crossing the farms, houses, and forests; slowly ascending the acclivities of the mountains; gradually sliding over the summits; and thus fading, successively, from sight. The contrast between the gloom and the splendour was so strong; the splendour itself was in many instances so vivid (for the spots were not equally bright and on that account were, in a group, more beautiful) that they appeared as if the vallies, farms, forests, and mountains, were successively polished and luminous. I never beheld any prospect more striking, or more complete.

—Timothy Dwight, 1798

The farm we have purchased is in a retired spot upon the brow of a large hill about one mile from the [West] Brattleborough meeting house. We have wheat and rye now in the ground and promising a sufficiency of those grains for our bread and pies. We have two large orchards and two smaller ones coming on, and expect to make some fifty or sixty barrels of cider. We have plenty of good pasturing and hay enough to winter thirty head of cattle. With the farm we purchased farming tools, young cattle, hogs, poultry, and twenty-three sheep who have now increased the flock by eight lambs, and it would amuse you to see Sophia and the children surrounded with sheep, lambs, geese, turkeys and hens, feeding them from their hands.

The house [has] a handsome portico, two handsome front rooms, well finished, papered and painted, and two handsome chambers over them; back is a sitting-room and by the side of it a room for my office, back of the sitting-room a good kitchen, from whence you go into two bed-rooms, one for the boys and the other for the maids, and overhead a meal granary; and over the sitting-room an apartment for our hired man and boy. Back of the kitchen is a long woodhouse, about twenty feet of which makes a summer washroom, and here stands the water-trough, constantly supplied with plenty of excellent water.

In front of the house is a fruit garden, peaches, plums, etc., but the former will not bear until

state in a large green and white hotel, fitted up for the accommodation of those who come to drink certain mineral waters of some repute in the neighbourhood. The season is over, and we occupied alone the "banquet-hall deserted." Here, though the rooms looked a little cold and empty at first, the good people soon made us very comfortable with tea and a good fire. The landlord, a thorough Yankee, received us in his bar with his feet on a high stove, his chair thrown back on its hind-legs, a cigar in his mouth, one eye shut, and his hat on. He was rather cool and contemptuous at first but softened by degrees and ended by treating us very well; so much so indeed that the next morning when we got up to go out shooting at four o'clock, though it was bitterly cold, he insisted upon getting up too and giving us our breakfast before we started.

The morning proved so stormy that the "hunters" with whom we had made an appointment could not bring over their boat, and though we paddled about for some time in two wretched little punts, about as seaworthy as a washing-tub, we got very few shots, as we were afraid to venture into deep water. The plan adopted by the hunters here is to paddle in one of these little punts, which do very well for one person through grass and reeds; and after waiting perhaps half a day they get a shot at a flock sitting and kill a dozen or more. They never shoot flying and hardly ever at a single bird, so that nothing can be more different than their idea of sport and ours. These pot-hunters express great surprise that a man who can afford to buy game should take the trouble to hunt it.

— *Joseph Robert Godley, 1842*

Near Newfane, by Arthur Griffin

Flaming Maples, Chelsea, by John H. Vondell

Green River Village, Guilford, by A. C. Shelton

Birch and Cherry, below, by Ernest Gay

Vershire, by Jack Breed

Bromley Mountain, by Gene Ahrens

Maple-lined Road, West Barnet, by Winston Pote

Lower Waterford Sugarhouse, by Dick Smith

Dead Creek, Addison, by Hanson Carroll

Camel's Hump, from Waterbury Center, by Dick Smith

Ottauquechee River, by Abner Kodess

Norwich Sunset, by Hanson Carroll

Frosty Elm, Thetford, by Gladys W. Estabrook

View near Waitsfield, by Ozzie Sweet

was happy to point out to us was several of our own flotilla [the British fleet from the Battle of Plattsburg] anchored near the town, sad "trophies of the fight".

At Shoreham, nearly opposite to Crown Point, we found good accommodation for the night at Mr. Larenburg's tavern, and set off the next morning before breakfast; but we had soon cause to repent of thus committing ourselves to the mercy of the elements. The lake now began to widen, and the shores to sink in the same proportion; the keen blasts of the north, sweeping over its frozen expanse, pierced us with needles of ice; the thermometer was 22° below zero; buffalo hides, bear skins, caps, shawls and handkerchiefs were vainly employed against a degree of cold so much beyond our habits. Our guide, alone of the party, his chin and eyelashes gemmed and powdered with the drifting snow, boldly set his face and his horses in the teeth of the storm. Sometimes a crack in the ice would compel us to wait, while he went forward to explore it with his axe (without which the American sleigh-drivers seldom travel) when, having ascertained its breadth and the foothold on either side, he would drive his horses at speed and clear the fissure, with its snow ridge, at a flying leap; a sensation we found agreeable enough, but not so agreeable as a good inn and dinner at Burlington.

— *Francis Hall, 1816*

Morning Frost at Marshfield, by Bruce O. Nett

Barnet Center,
by Carsten W. Johnson

Tobogganing,
by Ernest Gay

Near Weston, by Bullaty-Lomeo

Skating, Brattleboro, by Ernest Gay

South Pomfret,
by David Lawlor

Ski Trail at Killington, by Hanson Carroll

At Cambridge, by Winston Pote

In the Winter of 1965, i
of outside suggestion
Supreme Court, Vermon
its Legislature. By this o
phrenic struggle between
ing was largely remedie
Ralph E. Flanders had
trauma in the late 1700s
mont I have, in the bac
history, a case in which
linquished. Vermont was
which were independent
the Union. The instinct
demand that we give up
eignty. We should not giv
when and to the extent th
(*or local*) interest should

But what now was th
physical self? The early
Vermont "did their full
village industrialists, engi
have done theirs in the
Storrs Lee just before th
mistically felt that "Verm
verdure of the Green Mou
the obsessions and idiosy
those mountains."

As then-Governor Phili
however, to the newly ap
"Vermont has historically
cally as well as geographic
true. And, despite our res
cannot act as though it is
are more and more thr
sprawling cities and subu
south of us. Our lakes, ri

North Windham,
by John Harris

At Danville, by Winston Pote

Cross-country Skiing, Hartford, by Hanson Carroll

Missisquoi River near Sheldon Jct., by Winston Pote

Mt. Mansfield Ridge,
by Clyde Smith

Dummerston Brook, by John H. Vondell